LITERATURE
WORKS

A Collection of Readings

COLLECTION 1/3

Silver Burdett Ginn
A Division of Simon & Schuster
160 Gould Street
Needham Heights, MA 02194

Acknowledgments appear on page 224, which constitutes an extension of this copyright page.

© 1997 Silver Burdett Ginn Inc.
Center illustration this page from *George Shrinks* by William Joyce.

ISBN: 0-663-61218-7   4 5 6 7 8 9 10 RRD 03 02 01 00 99 98 97

LITERATURE WORKS

A Collection of Readings

COLLECTION 1 / 3

THEMES

Just Imagine

Changes in the Weather

SILVER BURDETT GINN

Needham, MA   Parsippany, NJ
Atlanta, GA   Deerfield, IL   Irving, TX   Santa Clara, CA

Theme 5

JUST IMAGINE

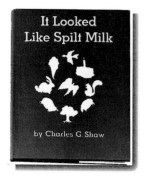

4

Theme 6

CHANGES IN THE WEATHER

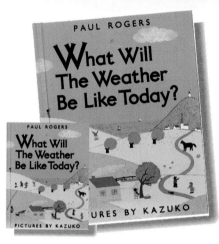

6

Just Imagine

Contents

Meet
Charles G. Shaw

Charles G. Shaw was a writer and a painter. Here is a picture of Mr. Shaw with one of his paintings. What does this painting look like to you?

It Looked Like Spilt Milk

by Charles G. Shaw

Sometimes it looked
like Spilt Milk.
But it wasn't Spilt Milk.

Sometimes it looked
like a Rabbit.
But it wasn't a Rabbit.

Sometimes it looked
like a Bird.
But it wasn't a Bird.

Sometimes it looked
like a Tree.
But it wasn't a Tree.

Sometimes it looked
like an Ice Cream Cone.
But it wasn't an Ice Cream Cone.

Sometimes it looked
like a Flower.
But it wasn't a Flower.

Sometimes it looked
like a Pig.
But it wasn't a Pig.

Sometimes it looked
like a Birthday Cake.
But it wasn't a Birthday Cake.

Sometimes it looked
like a Sheep.
But it wasn't a Sheep.

Sometimes it looked
like a Great Horned Owl.
But it wasn't a Great Horned Owl.

Sometimes it looked
like a Mitten.
But it wasn't a Mitten.

Sometimes it looked
like a Squirrel.
But it wasn't a Squirrel.

Sometimes it looked
like an Angel.
But it wasn't an Angel.

Sometimes it looked
like Spilt Milk.
But it wasn't Spilt Milk.
It was just a Cloud in the Sky.

What do clouds look like to you?
Draw a picture of clouds.
Write or tell about the clouds.

Cloud

The sky is clear,
And the cloud becomes
an airplane
Or a ship
Or a wave
And moves
And stops.
And I want to ride
On a cloud
And visit many places.

by Sueo Hyodo

Clouds Tell Us About the Weather

On sunny days you see light, fluffy clouds.

42   **When it rains, you see thick, gray clouds.**

What do these clouds tell about the weather?

Meet the Author and Illustrator

Dear Reader,

I wrote **EEK! There's a Mouse in the House** for my daughter, Ellen. She wanted me to write a story about her stuffed animals. She likes the story. I hope you do, too.

Wong Herbert Yee

Wong Herbert Yee

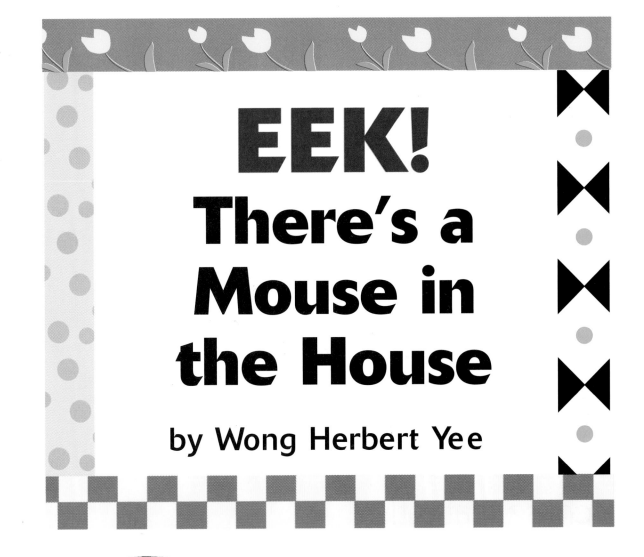

EEK!
There's a Mouse in the House

by Wong Herbert Yee

45

EEK!

There's a Mouse in the house.

Send in the Cat
to chase that rat!

Uh-oh!

The Cat knocked over a lamp.

Send in the Dog
to catch that scamp!

Dear me!

The Dog has broken a dish.

And now the Cat is after the fish.

Send in the Hog
to shoo that Dog!

Oh my!

The Hog is eating the cake.

Sending the Hog
was a big mistake.

Send in the Cow.

Send that Cow NOW!

Oh no!

The Cow is dancing
with a mop.

Send in the Sheep
to make her stop!

Goodness!

The Sheep is tangled in yarn.

Send in the Hen from the barn!

Mercy!

The Hen is laying eggs
on the table.

Send in the Horse
from the stable!

Heavens!

The Horse kicked a hole
in the wall.

Send in the Elephant
to get rid of them ALL!

The Elephant was BIG,
but he squeezed through the door.
Once he was in,
there was room for no more.

Out of the house marched the Cat and the Cow.

Out came the Horse and the Hen and the Hog.

Out walked the Sheep.

Out ran the Dog.

But then from within,
there came a shout:

EEK! There's a Mouse in the house!

Draw a silly picture about a mouse in your house.

Write a sentence to tell about your drawing.

Elephant

by
Langston Hughes

animal sculptures by students from
the Harlem School of the Arts

Elephant,
Elephant,
Big as a
House!

They tell me
That you
Are afraid of a
Mouse.

Meet William Joyce

William Joyce likes to draw funny pictures for children. Grown-ups like his pictures, too!

Here is a picture William Joyce drew of himself.

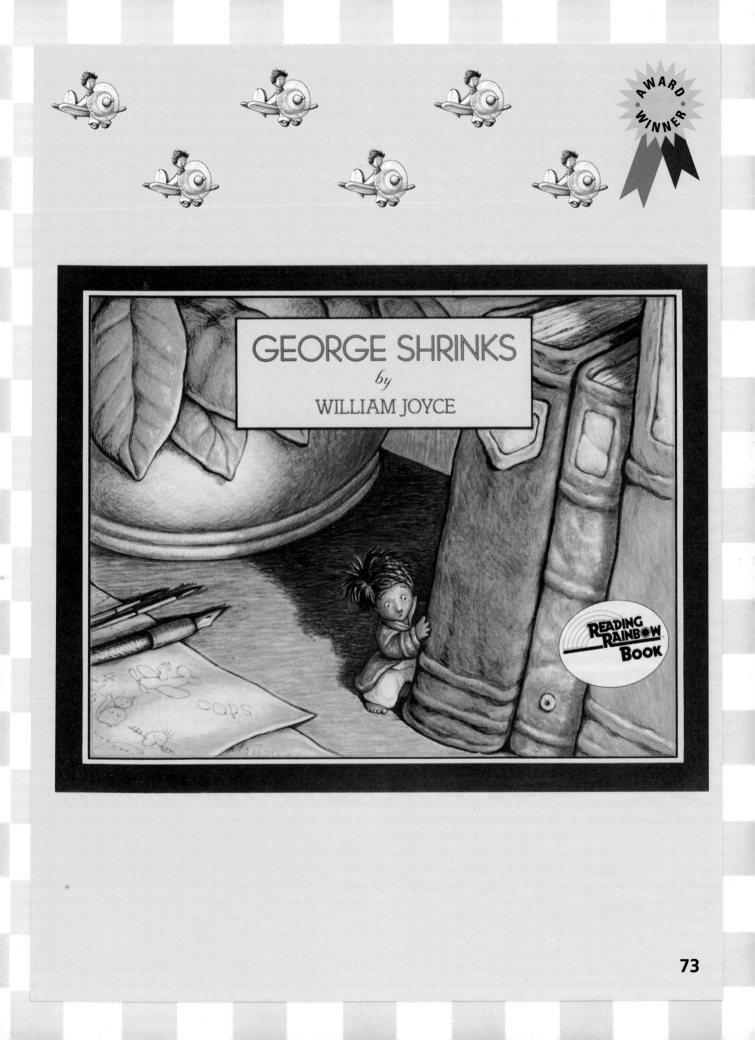

GEORGE SHRINKS

by

WILLIAM JOYCE

One day, while his mother and father were out, George dreamt he was small, and when he woke up he found it was true.

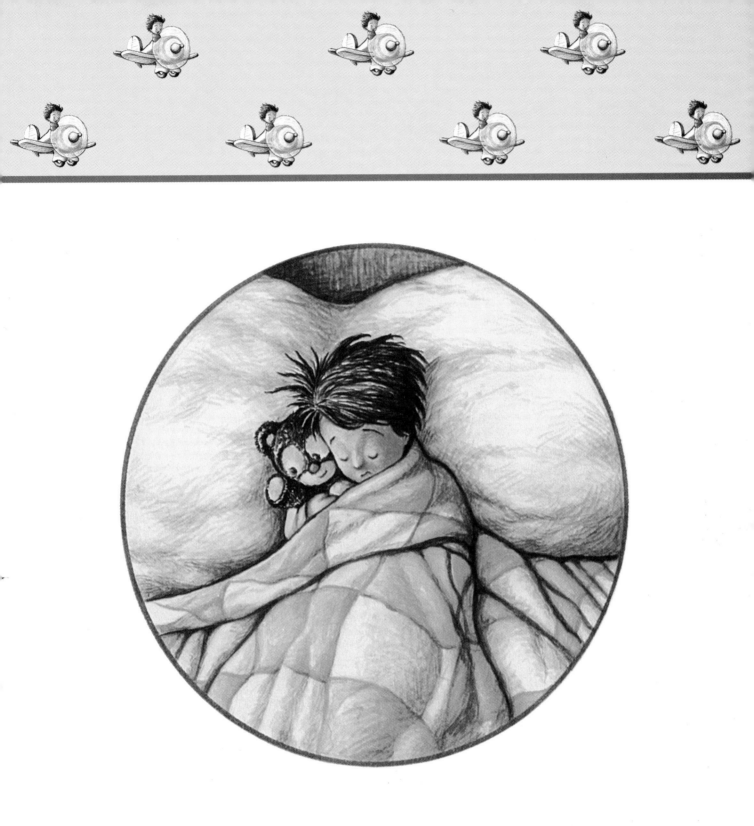

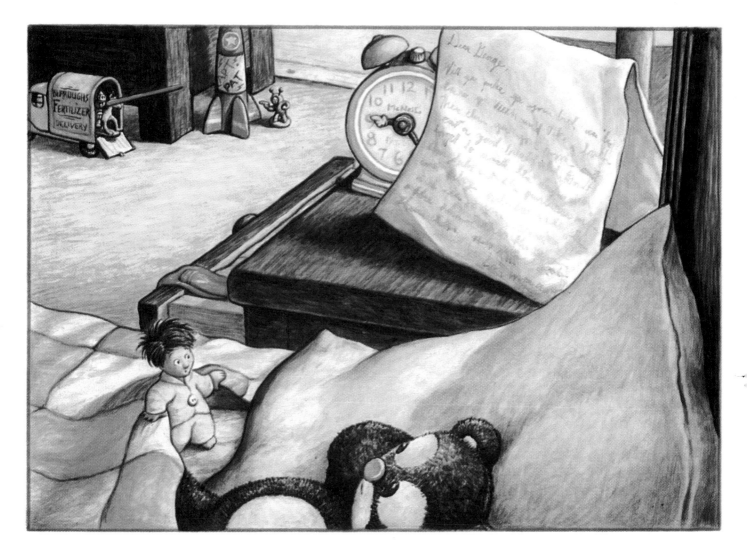

His parents had left him a note:

"Dear George," it said. "When you wake up,

please make your bed,

brush your teeth,

and take a bath.

Then clean up your room

and go get your little brother.

Eat a good breakfast,

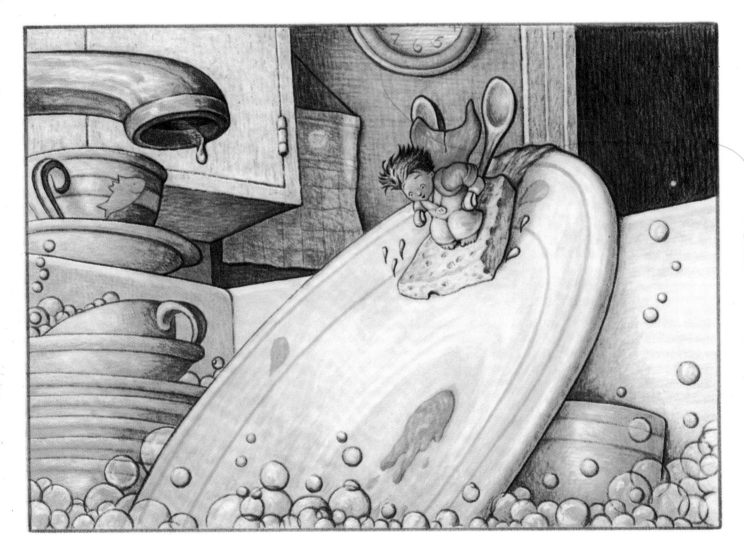

and don't forget to wash the dishes, dear.

Take out the garbage,

and play quietly.

Make sure you water the plants

and feed the fish.

Then check the mail

and get some fresh air.

Try to stay out of trouble,

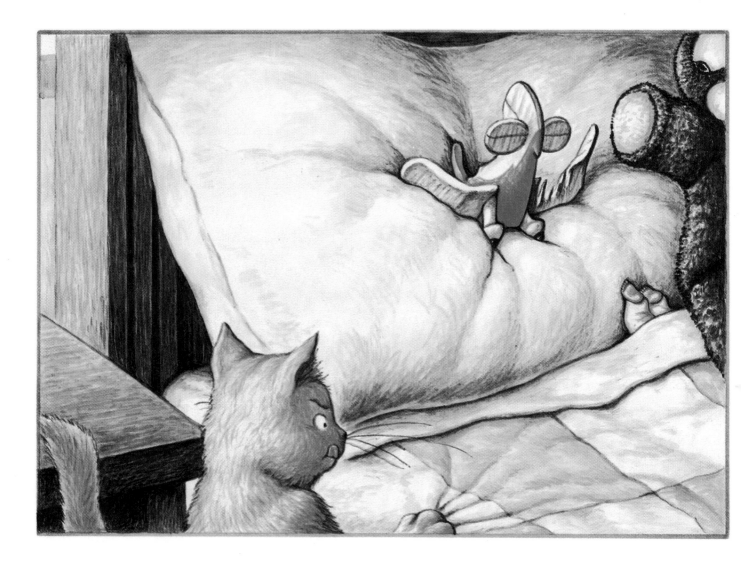

and we'll be home soon.

Love, Mom and Dad."

Pretend you are as small as George.

Where would you sleep?

What would you eat?

Draw a picture to show your ideas.

101

♥ MY BED ♥

1. I am the king in my castle.

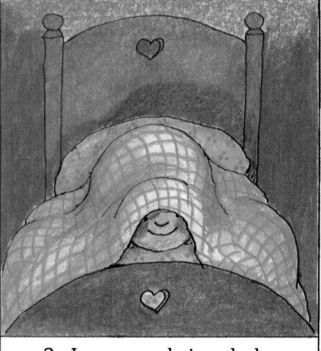

2. I am a mole in a hole.

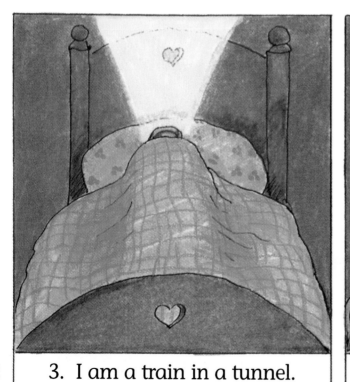

3. I am a train in a tunnel.

4. I am a pirate in a den.

102

by Franz Brandenberg
illustrated by Aliki

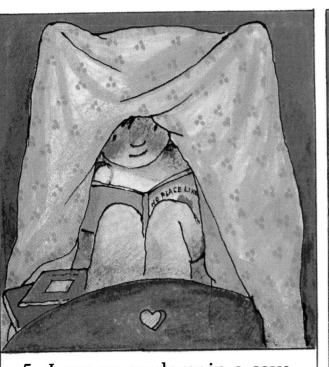

5. I am an explorer in a cave.

6. I am a lion tamer in a circus tent.

7. I am a bear asleep in my lair.

8. Good night.

Theme Trade Book

Any Kind of Dog

by Lynn Reiser, Greenwillow Books, 1992

Richard wants a real dog, not a pretend dog! Will Richard's wish ever come true?

More Books for You to Enjoy

The Glerp
by David McPhail, Silver Press, 1995

The Glerp eats anything that gets in his way. What will the Glerp do when he meets an elephant?

One Monday Morning
by Uri Shulevitz, Aladdin Books, 1974

A king, a queen, and other imaginary friends try to visit a little boy. The friends return every day until the boy is home to greet them.

Fortunately
by Remy Charlip, Aladdin Books, 1993

Ned has a wild adventure on his way to a birthday party.

Changes in the Weather

Contents

Tomie dePaola

Tomie dePaola started drawing when he was two years old. Since then he has made over two hundred books! He likes to write stories and then draw the pictures to go with them. Sometimes he gets his story ideas from his family.

THE WIND AND THE SUN

retold and illustrated by
Tomie dePaola

The wind and the sun were
talking. Who was stronger?

They saw a man walking below.

"I will show you I am stronger,"
said the wind. "I will blow the
cape from that man."

The wind began to blow.

The wind blew as hard as it could.

But the man held the cape
around him as tightly as he
could.

The wind stopped.

"Now," said the sun, "it is my turn."
The sun began to shine.
It began to get warm.

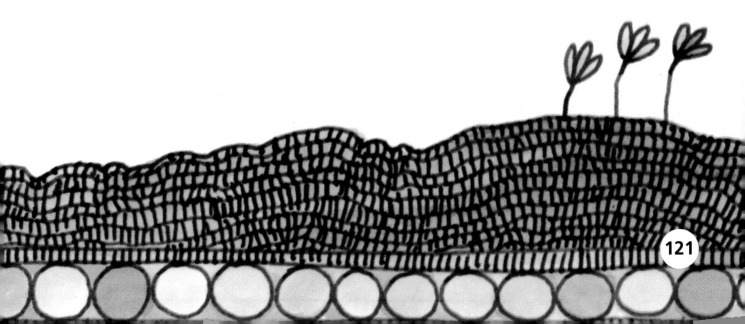

Then it became very warm.

At last it was hot.

The man took off his cape and
went to sit in the shade of a tree.

"You see," said the sun to the wind.

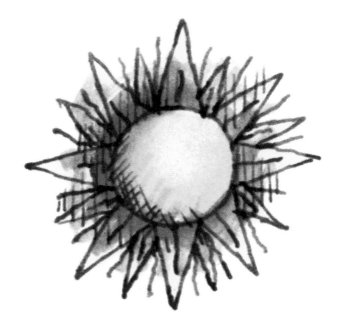

And that is how the sun
showed it was stronger.

Pretend you are the sun.

Have a friend pretend to be the wind.

Tell why the sun and the wind are important.

Draw pictures to show your ideas.

How the Sun Was Born

Cómo el Sol Nació

**written and illustrated by third-grade art students
at Drexel Elementary School, Tucson, Arizona**

AWARD WINNER

Hace muchos, muchos años una mamá dinosauria puso cinco huevos. Ella los enterró en la arena tibia.

Many many years ago a mother dinosaur laid five eggs.
She buried them in the warm sand.

Después de diez días todos nacieron, con la excepción de uno.   Éste se quedó bajo tierra.
Los volcanes empezaron a hacer erupción. La ardiente lava roja cubrió la tierra y todos los dinosaurios murieron.

After ten days they all hatched except one.
This one stayed under the sand.
Volcanos started to erupt. The red hot lava covered the land and killed all the dinosaurs.

La arena en la tierra se puso más y más caliente. El huevo solitario se puso tan caliente que se abrió y nació el bebé dinosaurio. Se transformó en una bola de fuego.

The sand in the earth became hotter and hotter. The lonely dinosaur egg became very hot and it hatched. The baby dinosaur turned into a ball of fire.

El calor de la lava hizo que se levantara hacia el cielo.
Ésta se convirtió en el sol.

**The heat from the lava made it glide up into the sky.
This became the sun.**

En la noche, cuando la obscuridad entra, él regresa a su huevo debajo de la arena.
Así es cómo el sol vino a nacer.

**At night, when it is dark, it returns to its egg under the sand.
This is how the sun was born.**

Meet the authors of **How the Sun Was Born**

These third-grade children wrote **How the Sun Was Born**. They worked together to make up the story. Their art teacher helped them make the drawings. The children go to the Drexel Elementary School in Tucson, Arizona.

Mary Serfozo

Mary Serfozo won a writing contest when she was in the fifth grade. She has always loved to write. She likes the sound of words like "ping" and "ploomp" in **Rain Talk**. Her hobbies are travel and photography.

Keiko Narahashi

Keiko Narahashi got her ideas for **Rain Talk** in North Carolina, where she grew up. She lived in the country where the ground was made of red clay. When it rained, she loved the way the wet clay felt between her toes.

RAIN TALK

Mary Serfozo
illustrated by Keiko Narahashi

Ploomp go the first fat raindrops,

Ploomp Ploomp Ploomp
into the soft summer dust
of a country road.

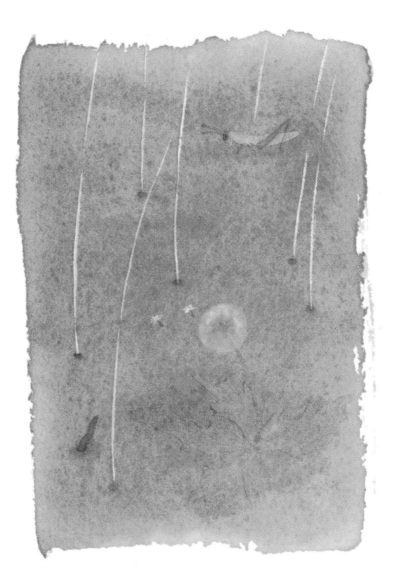

Each little drop digs a dark little hole
and the smell of wet dust tickles my nose.

On the old tin roof of the garden shed
the drops all try to talk at once . . .
Ping Ping PingaDing
Ping Ping Ping Ping Ping . . .

and they chuckle together
as they run down the drain.

It's raining harder now.
Listen to the
PlipPlipPlipPlipPlipPlip
as it speckles the smooth surface of the pond.

To Mother Duck
that says,
"Time to go for a swim."

Out on the highway
the raindrops bounce high,
and *Whoosh* and *Hiss*
as the cars hurry by.

Headlights are coming on,
reaching out to catch
the silvery slants of rain.

Now all I can hear
is the *Bup Bup Bup Bup*
of rain thumping on my umbrella . . .

and dropping and dripping all around.

Mother says to come in the house
and the rain tries to come in too ...
*Flick ... Flick ... Flick*ing itself
like pebbles against the windowpanes.

I'd rather stay outside.

When I've had my supper and bath
I lie in front of the fire. And now and then
a raindrop slips down the chimney
to *Spit* and *Sizzle* on the logs.

I'm getting very sleepy here.

Tucked into my bed upstairs
I try to stay awake and listen to the
Drum-a-tum-a-Drum-a-tum-a-Drum-a-tum
on the roof above my head.

But my eyes . . . just won't . . . stay . . . open.

Tomorrow I may find the rain all gone,
with only a sparkle still caught
in a spiderweb or a flower.

But I'll look first . . .

for a rainbow!

What does a windy day sound like?

What does a thunderstorm sound like?

Draw some weather pictures.

Make sounds to go with your pictures.

from
Grandmother's Nursery Rhymes

translated from the Spanish
by Nelly Palacio Jaramillo, illustrated by Elivia

The Clouds
Sprinklers that are bigger
Than the great, big sun,
Sprinkling the earth
Until the harvest's done.

The Wind
I whistle without lips,
I fly without wings,
I clap without hands
And touch all living things.

The Sun in Art

Vincent van Gogh,
Dutch, *Olive Trees with Yellow Sky and Sun*, 1889
The Minneapolis Institute of Arts

Huichol Indian Yarn Painting of Sun,
Mexican, 1978

Manuscript,
Italian, 15th Century

Meet Robert Maass

Robert Maass wanted to show what summer is like in the city and in the country. During the summer he grows flowers and vegetables in his backyard garden in Brooklyn, New York. He also enjoys fishing in the country.

When Summer Comes

by Robert Maass

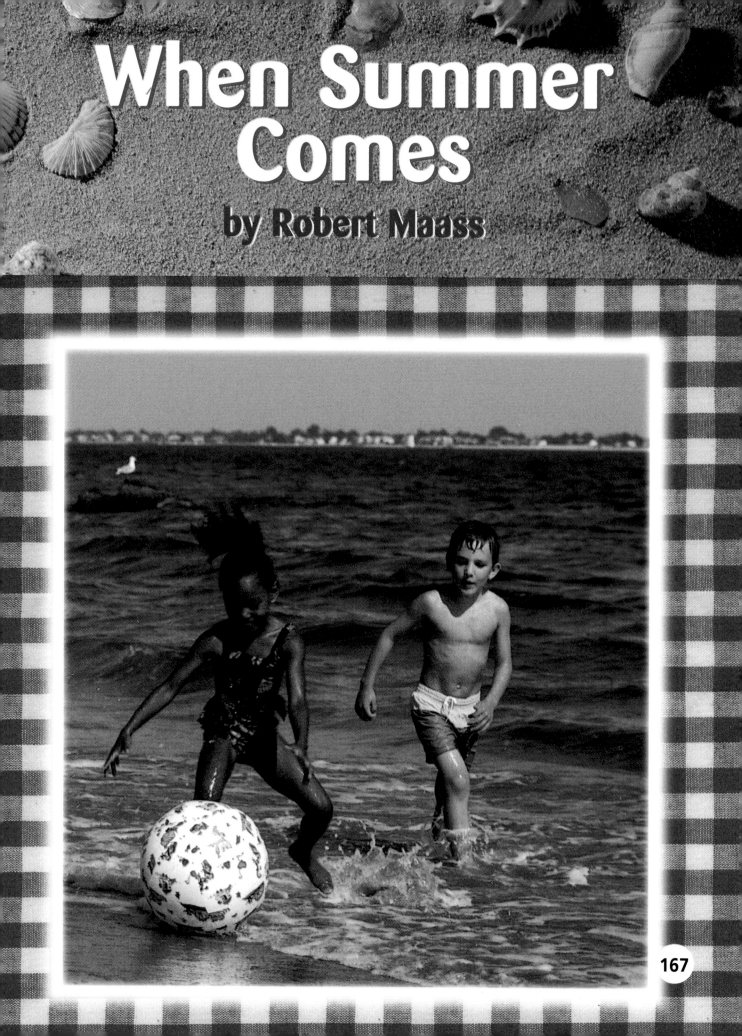

When school lets out

and sun pours down . . .

that's when summer comes.

Early in summer the first fruits
are ripe for eating.

Fresh-picked vegetables appear at
roadside stands.

Fifers march
and fireworks flare

when the corn's knee-high
on the Fourth of July.

Bugs wake up when summer comes.
Caterpillars crawl, butterflies alight,
Water-skippers cast shadows
in ponds. Fat bees hover.

Water's best in summertime. Cool and clear,

it gushes from a sprinkler or tosses breezes at the beach

or swirls in a rushing stream.

It's also the place to catch fish.

Summer is a time for street
fairs sandwiched between
city buildings.

The hot summer night is
filled with brassy music,
lights, and magic.

Country fairs under bright summer skies
mean food and games and fun, a place
to show prize animals
(or take a break in the shade).

Baseball makes summer dreams come true.

When summer comes, a hot dog from the grill
or a slice of juicy watermelon
is better than a fancy meal.

There's money to be made,

and money to be spent.

Summer is a time for new experiences

and old-fashioned pleasures.

When the last stalks tower and the flowers
are full-blown,

it's time to gather summer's late harvest.

There's one more swing to try,

one more ride to take,

and one more day at the beach. Then, much
too soon, a cool breeze blows,
and summer slips away.

It's hard to say good-bye to summer.

What do you like to do
when summer comes?

Tell about one of your
summer days.

Share some summer
pictures with a friend.

How to Build a
SAND CASTLE

You need:

- wet, smooth sand
- a shovel
- a bucket
- a wooden block

Directions:

1. Build a very big sand pile.
2. Pack the sand down with your hands.
3. Make the top of the sand pile flat.
4. Make towers on the sand pile.
5. Carve out windows, gates, or bridges.

What else could you make with sand?

Theme Trade Book

The Wind Blew

by Pat Hutchins, Aladdin Books, 1993

When the wind blew, it took a balloon, a hat, some letters, a kite, and even a wig with it!

More Books for You to Enjoy

Ska-tat!

by Kimberley Knutson, Macmillan, 1993

Three friends enjoy playing in the colorful fall leaves.

Snowed In

by Barbara M. Lucas, illustrated by Catherine Stock, Bradbury Press, 1993

Winter storms keep a family on their farm. Everyone keeps busy all winter long.

Storm's Coming

by Dave and Julie Saunders, Bradbury Press, 1994

Two squirrels find themselves far from their home in a tree when a storm comes. Where will they hide?

GLOSSARY

around

Around means on all sides or in a circle. Fred drew a line **around** the picture.

birthday

Birthday means having to do with celebrating the day one is born. Sara had a big **birthday** party with all her friends.

birthday

breakfast

Breakfast is the first meal of the day. If you eat a good **breakfast**, you will feel good all day.

breakfast

broken

Broken means having caused something to split or crack into pieces. The cat had **broken** the dish when she knocked it over.

broken

brother

A **brother** is a boy or man who has the same parents as other children in the family. My **brother** takes care of my sisters when our parents are at work.

cape

A **cape** is a piece of cloth worn as a coat. The man liked to wear his long, red **cape** on windy days.

cape

211

chimney

A **chimney** is a place where smoke from the fireplace goes out of the house. On cold winter days, you can see smoke coming out of the **chimney.**

chimney

chuckle

Chuckle means to laugh quietly. Sam began to **chuckle** when he heard the joke.

dancing

Dancing means moving the body and feet in a pattern, usually to music. The children like **dancing** in a circle.

dancing

drain

A **drain** is a pipe that carries off water
The outside **drain** carried away much
of the rainwater.

dust

Dust is small, light, dry bits of dirt.
The **dust** in the air made him sneeze.

drain

experiences

Experiences are special things a person
has done. We had many new **experiences**
when we visited our grandmother's farm.

fairs

Fairs are special events where people buy and
sell things. Sometimes, people show their best
animals and crops. Some **fairs** have rides,
games, and shows. In the summer, my brother
and I love to go on rides at the **fair**.

fair

POPCORN

DRINKS

fireworks

fireworks

Fireworks are bursts of fire and light that explode in the sky. We had to cover our ears when the bright **fireworks** made a loud bang.

Gg

garbage

Garbage is scraps of food or other things that are thrown away. They threw away the **garbage** after they ate their dinner.

garbage

gushes

Gushes means pours out with force and in large amounts. The water **gushes** out of the pipe when it rains.

gushes

Hh

harvest

Harvest is the planted fruit, vegetables, and grain that are ready to be picked. In the fall, the farmer picked the rest of his **harvest.**

harvest

hover

Hover means to hang or flutter in the air over something. The dark clouds **hover** over the town before the storm.

Ii

ice cream

Ice cream is a frozen food made with cream or milk, sugar, and flavorings. Many people love to eat **ice cream** on a hot day.

ice cream

215

kicked

Kicked means hit or struck with the foot. She **kicked** the soccer ball into the net.

kicked

Mm

march

March means to take high, even steps in a line or row. The high school band will **march** in our town parade.

mistake

A **mistake** is something one does that is wrong. When I made a **mistake** on my paper, my teacher helped me fix it.

mitten

A **mitten** is something to wear on your hand when it is cold. Ben lost his **mitten** when he went sledding.

mitten

new

New means seen, made, or thought of for the first time. He looked at the shiny, **new** bike in the store window.

pond

ponds

Ponds are small lakes. Ducks like to swim on small **ponds**.

quietly

Quietly means softly. They talked very **quietly** when the baby was sleeping.

rainbow

A **rainbow** is a curved band of many colors that sometimes appears in the sky after it rains. We saw a beautiful **rainbow** in the sky.

rainbow

ripe

A **ripe** fruit or vegetable is one that is ready to be picked and eaten. The **ripe** peach was sweet and juicy.

shade

Shade is cover from the sun. The man sat in the **shade** under the big tree.

shade

shed

A **shed** is a small building where tools and other things are stored. The family keeps their bikes in the **shed** in their backyard.

shed

218

shout

A **shout** is a sudden, loud cry or call.
You could hear a **shout** from the coach
at the other end of the field.

shrinks

Shrinks means to get smaller. This kind of
shirt **shrinks** when you put it in the dryer.

shrinks

sparkle

A **sparkle** is a little flash of light.
The **sparkle** of the ring caught my eye.

sparkle

squeezed

Squeezed means pushed or pressed. The fat mouse **squeezed** through the small hole.

squirrel

A **squirrel** is a small animal with a bushy tail that eats nuts and lives in trees. The **squirrel** made a nest in the tree.

squirrel

stable

A **stable** is a place where horses and cows are kept. Kelly walked her horse back to the **stable** when she was done riding.

stable

stalks stalks

Stalks are long plant stems. The tall corn **stalks** were lined up in rows like soldiers.

swirls

Swirls means turns around and around. The leaf **swirls** around and around as it falls to the ground.

swirls

- -

tangled

Tangled means to have become twisted or knotted. The girl's comb got **tangled** in her long hair.

tickles

Tickles means to touch someone in a way that makes them laugh. The soft feather **tickles** my nose.

221

tightly

Tightly means fitting closely or held firmly. The boy wrapped the blanket around himself so **tightly** that he didn't feel the cold air.

trouble

Trouble is a problem caused by doing something you are not supposed to do. The puppy got into **trouble** when he chewed on the chair.

umbrella

An **umbrella** is something that is used to keep one dry when it is raining. The girl opened the **umbrella** when she felt the raindrops.

umbrella

vegetables

Vegetables are plants such as beans, peas, and squash that can be eaten raw or cooked. The farmer picked fresh **vegetables** from his fields every day.

vegetables

Volcanos are mountains with openings where hot, melted rock pours out. The people who lived in the village below the **volcanos** were afraid they would have to leave their homes.

volcano

walked

Walked means went on foot. The friends **walked** to the store after school.

watermelon

A **watermelon** is a large fruit that is green on the outside and red on the inside. The father cut the big, round **watermelon** into juicy, red slices.

watermelon

---

yarn

yarn

Yarn is a kind of string used to knit sweaters and other warm clothes. My mother used blue **yarn** to knit me a hat and mittens.

ACKNOWLEDGMENTS

Grateful acknowledgment is made to the following publishers, authors, and agents for their permission to reprint copyrighted material. Every effort has been made to locate all copyright proprietors; any errors or omissions in copyright notice are inadvertent and will be corrected in future printings as they are discovered.

"Cloud" by Sueo Hyodo from **We Wrote These Poems**. Edited by Takeshi Nakano and Naoshi Koriyama. Translated by Naoshi Koriyama. ©1982 Hokuseido Press, Tokyo, 1982. Reprinted by permission of Naoshi Koriyama.

"The Clouds" from **Grandmother's Nursery Rhymes/Las Nanas de Abuelita** by Nelly Palacio Jaramillo. Illustrated by Elivia Savadier. Text copyright ©1994 by Nelly Palacio Jaramillo. Illustrations copyright ©1994 by Elivia Savadier. Reprinted by permission of Henry Holt and Co., Inc.

EEK! There's a Mouse in the House by Wong Herbert Yee. Copyright ©1992 by Wong Herbert Yee. Reprinted by permission of Houghton Mifflin Co. All rights reserved.

"Elephant" from **The Sweet and Sour Animal Book** by Langston Hughes. Illustrations by students from the Harlem School of the Arts. Text copyright ©1994 by Ramona Bass and Arnold Rampersad, Administrators of the Estate of Langston Hughes. Illustrations copyright ©1994 by Oxford University Press, Inc. Reprinted by permission of Oxford University Press, Inc.

George Shrinks by William Joyce. Illustrated by William Joyce. Copyright ©1985 by William Joyce. Reprinted by permission of HarperCollins Publishers.

How the Sun Was Born/Cómo el Sol Nació written and illustrated by third-grade art students at Drexel Elementary School, Tucson, Arizona. Copyright ©1993 by Willowisp Press Inc. Published by arrangement with Willowisp Press, Inc., 801 94th Avenue North, St. Petersburg, Florida 33702. Additional information regarding the Kids Are Authors Program may be obtained by calling 1-800-726-8090.

It Looked Like Spilt Milk by Charles G. Shaw. Copyright 1947 by Charles G. Shaw. Renewed 1975 by Ethan Allen. Reprinted by permission of HarperCollins Publishers.

"My Bed" by Franz Brandenberg. Illustrated by Aliki. Text copyright ©1992 by Franz Brandenberg. Illustrations copyright ©1992 by Aliki. Taken from **Home**, edited by Michael J. Rosen. Copyright ©1992 by HarperCollins Publishers. Reprinted by permission of Share Our Strength.

Phonetic respelling system from **The World Book Encyclopedia**. ©1995 World Book, Inc. By permission of the publisher.

Rain Talk by Mary Serfozo. Illustrations by Keiko Narahashi. Text copyright ©1990 by Mary Serfozo. Illustrations copyright ©1990 by Keiko Narahashi. Reprinted with permission of Margaret K. McElderry Books, Simon & Schuster Children's Publishing Division.

When Summer Comes by Robert Maass. Copyright ©1993 by Robert Maass. Reprinted by permission of Henry Holt and Co., Inc.

"The Wind" from **Grandmother's Nursery Rhymes/Las Nanas de Abuelita** by Nelly Palacio Jaramillo. Illustrated by Elivia Savadier. Text copyright ©1994 by Nelly Palacio Jaramillo. Illustrations copyright ©1994 by Elivia Savadier. Reprinted by permission of Henry Holt and Co., Inc.

COVER: Cover photograph ©1996 by Jade Albert Studio. Cover illustration ©1996 by Mary Jane Begin. Cover design, art direction and production by Design Five.

ILLUSTRATION: 40, Mike Reed; 106–107, Michael Bryant.

GLOSSARY ILLUSTRATION: 210, Nan Brooks; 212, Eileen Hine; 213, Nan Brooks (Top), Philip Scheuer (Bottom); 214, Ramune (Top), Eileen Hine (Middle), Kat Thacker (Bottom); 215, Meryl Brenner; 216, Christa Kieffer; 217, Ramune; 218, Meryl Brenner; 219, Roz Schanzer; 220, Carol Inouye; 221, Meryl Brenner (Top), Ramune (Bottom); 222–223, Kat Thacker.

PHOTOGRAPHY: Unless otherwise indicated, photographs of book covers and of children's art were provided by Ulsaker Studio, Inc. Background photograph for Silver Bookcase by Allan Penn for SBG. Credits listed below for children's art indicate the name of the artist. The abbreviation SBG stands for Silver Burdett Ginn. 8–9, (all) Doug Mindell for SBG; 10, detail of photo from the Charles G. Shaw papers, Archives of American Art, Smithsonian Institution, photo by Charles H. Phillips; 10–11, © Mark Romanelli/The Image Bank; 41, (t.) © 1991 Luis Castañeda/The Image Bank, (b.) Doug Mindell for SBG; 42, (t.) © Donald Dietz/Stock·Boston, (b.) © 1984 Pamela J. Zilly/The Image Bank; 43, (t.) © Luis Castañeda/The Image Bank, (b.) © 1988 Steve Krongard/The Image Bank; 44, courtesy Wong Herbert Yee; 69, (t.) drawing by Adam Finelli, (b.) George Disario for SBG; 70, (t.) Doug Mindell for SBG; 72, (t. r.) courtesy HarperCollins Publishers, photo by Neil Johnson, (l.) courtesy HarperCollins Publishers; 108, © John Gilbert Fox; 138, (both) courtesy Simon & Schuster; 164, Vincent van Gogh, *Olive Trees*, The Minneapolis Institute of Arts; 165, (t.) © 1991 Girard Foundation Collection in the Museum of International Folk Art, a unit of the Museum of New Mexico, Santa Fe, New Mexico, photo by Mark Schwartz, (b.) Alinari/Regione Umbria/Art Resource, New York; 166, (b.) courtesy Henry Holt and Company; 166–167, Doug Mindell for SBG; 167–205, (border) Doug Mindell for SBG; 206, Doug Mindell for SBG; 207, (t., b.) courtesy of the American Institute of Architects, Houston, Texas, photos by Harold Smyser, (m.) © Joel Hoo, (r.) © Nancy Sheehan; 210, Allan Penn for SBG; 211, Dave Bradley for SBG; 212, 215, Doug Mindell for SBG; 216, Allan Penn for SBG; 219, Doug Mindell for SBG; 220, © Steve Maslowski/Photo Researchers, Inc.; 222, Allan Penn for SBG; 223, (t.) © F. Rossotto, USGS/Stocktrek/Tom Stack & Associates, (m.) Dave Bradley for SBG, (b.) Allan Penn for SBG.